PIONEER VALLEY EDUCATIONAL PRESS, INC

ICE SKATING

ROSE LEWIS

TABLE OF CONTENTS

People have been ice skating for many, many years. The first ice skates were made from animal bones. Leather straps were used to tie the skates on. Sometimes people needed sticks to push themselves around on the ice.

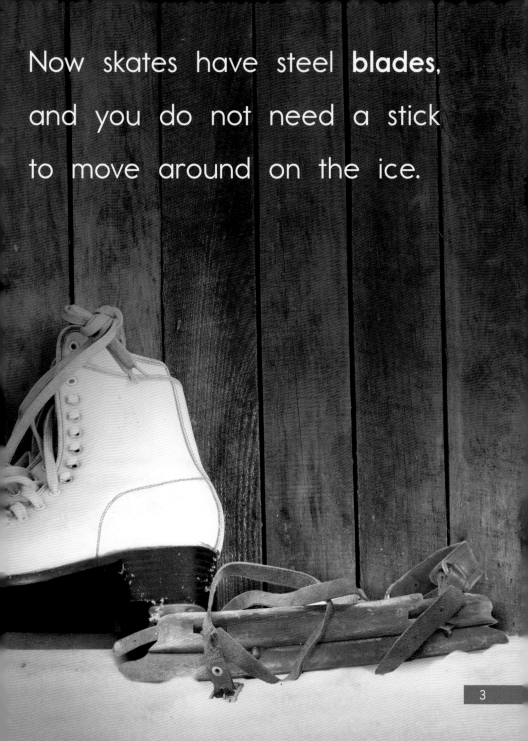

Now skates have steel **blades**, and you do not need a stick to move around on the ice.

Learning how to skate takes lots of practice and hard work. **Figure** skating is a mix of skating, dance, and gymnastics. Figure skaters do many turns, jumps, and lifts.

Many people like to skate on frozen lakes and ponds in the winter.

If you skate on a pond or a lake, make sure the ice is frozen and safe!

People can skate
in the summer, too!
When it is warm outside,
there are many indoor
ice skating rinks
where everyone can skate.

Ice skates are leather boots with steel blades on the bottom. Ice skates should fit well. Your foot should not move around in the boot when you are skating.

At the toe end of the blade is a jagged edge called a toe pick.

Before you can skate, you need to learn to walk on the ice. Then you will learn to **glide**.

A new skater can hold someone's hand or hold onto a chair to stay **balanced.**

Next, you can learn
how to stop,
skate backwards, spin,
and jump.

It takes a lot of practice
to learn how to spin
on the ice.

Jumping in the air and landing on the ice also takes a lot of skill and practice. There are many different kinds of jumps.

Sometimes two figure skaters skate together. This is called pair skating. The two skaters skate side by side and do lifts, spins, and jumps.

In a competition, judges give the skater points from zero to six. The judges give points on how well and how beautifully the skater skates.

balance: steady and even

blade: flat cutting part

figure: a form

glide: to move smoothly